Table of Contents

Decaying Democracy

The everyday struggles of the average American are often painful and overwhelming. The price of daily necessities is too expensive for the average paycheck to cover, leaving entire families sometimes to starve. The

GOVERNMENT, THOUGH
HAVING BEEN TOLD,
BARELY LISTENS, AND
INSTEAD CONTINUES TO
FEAST OFF THE BACKS OF
OUR HARD WORK.
CORRUPTION IS RAMPANT
AMONG BOTH THE
GOVERNMENT AND CIVIL
SERVICES. THOSE WHO
ARE MEANT TO PROTECT
US DO LITTLE TO CHANGE
OUR CONSTANT BATTLE
WITH STARVATION AND

SADNESS. THOSE WHO
SUFFER WITH MENTAL
ILLNESS ARE LEFT BY THE
GOVERNMENT TO FEND
FOR THEMSELVES AS OUR
LEADERS REFUSE TO PUT
FUNDING INTO THEIR
WELFARE.

DRUGS RUIN OUR
ONCE BEAUTIFUL CITIES
AND BOTH THE STATE AND
FEDERAL GOVERNMENTS
REFUSE TO HELP CHANGE

ANYTHING, LEAVING THE ORDINARY AMERICAN TO CONSTANTLY FEAR FOR NOT ONLY THEIR WELLBEING BUT ALSO THEIR FAMILY. CHILDREN AND ANIMALS PLAY IN THE STREETS THAT ARE CONSTANTLY COVERED IN DIRTY NEEDLES. IN CALIFORNIA, CRIMINALS ARE ALLOWED TO STEAL FROM SOMEBODY AND ARE GRANTED

PROTECTION BY THE
GOVERNMENT,
PREVENTING THE OWNER
OF SAID STOLEN
PROPERTY FROM
PROTECTING OR GETTING
IT BACK.

DURING TRAGEDIES IN
WHICH LARGE NUMBERS
OF PEOPLE LOSE THEIR
HOMES, SUCH AS
WILDFIRES, THE
GOVERNMENT SAYS THEY

WILL HELP US, YET IT IS
ALL A LIE. THEY NEVER
HELP US, THEY ONLY DO IT
TO CALM OUR
GRIEVANCES. INSTEAD,
THEY LEAVE THE PEOPLE
TO PICK UP THE PIECES OF
WHAT IS LEFT AND TRY TO
PUT IT BACK TOGETHER.
THESE VERY PEOPLE WHO
LOST EVERYTHING ARE
EXPECTED TO REPAIR
WHAT THEY NO LONGER
HAVE BECAUSE THE

GOVERNMENT REFUSES
TO PROVIDE A SINGLE
PENNY OF FUNDING.

THE AVERAGE
AMERICAN WORKERS
PAYCHECK IS OFTEN
BELOW THE AMOUNT
REQUIRED FOR LIVING.
INCOME INEQUALITY
CAUSED BY THE
STAGNATION OF MINIMUM
WAGE, THE WEAKENING
OF LABOR UNIONS, AND

GOVERNMENT POLICIES
ALL HURT THE WORKER.
OUTSOURCING CAUSES
MANY TO BE FIRED ALL TO
SAVE COSTS. THE
HOMELESS RATE
CONTINUES TO RISE AS
NOW AMERICAN
CIVILIANS ARE UNABLE TO
PAY BILLS AND ARE
FORCED OUT OF THEIR
HOMES AND INTO
SHELTERS.

OUR VETERANS ARE OFTEN TREATED POORLY BECAUSE OF THE COST OF HEALTHCARE AND LACK OF RECOGNITION OF MENTAL HEALTH AMONG THE AMERICAN POPULATION. THE GOVERNMENT DOESN'T HELP PAY FOR MENTAL HEALTH PROGRAMS, LEAVING MANY ALONE WITHOUT PROPER HELP. MANY VETERANS AREN'T

HIRED AS EMPLOYEES BECAUSE MANY EMPLOYERS DON'T WANT THEM BECAUSE OF THE INJURIES THEY RECEIVED IN THE CONFLICT THEY SERVED IN.

TODAY OUR NATION IS DIVIDED AMONG REPUBLICANS AND DEMOCRATS. DIVISION SLOWS PROGRESS TOWARDS UNIFICATION

AND ONLY THREATENS
OUR NATION'S SURVIVAL.
THE CAPITAL RIOTS
ALMOST TORE OUR
NATION APART BECAUSE
OF THE DIVISION AMONG
OUR PEOPLE. IT CAUSED
THE DEATH OF FIVE
PEOPLE. WE ALL KNOW
THAT DIVISION, IF LEFT TO
FESTER, CAN LEAD TO
CIVIL WAR. THE
AMERICAN CIVIL WAR
WAS THE BLOODIEST WAR

IN ALL AMERICAN
HISTORY, CLAIMING THE
LIVES OF 600,000
SOLDIERS. THAT IS MORE
THAN AMERICAN
CASUALTIES IN BOTH
WORLD WARS COMBINED.
THE CIVIL WAR WAS AND
STILL IS CALLED THE
BROTHERS WAR
BECAUSE IT WAS FOUGHT
AMONG AMERICANS. THE
WAR BROKE OUT
BECAUSE OF THE DEEP-

ROOTED DIVISION
BETWEEN NORTH AND
SOUTH, SLAVERY AND THE
FREED. IN THE END, IT LED
TO SEGREGATIONIST
LAWS AND THE
FORMATION OF THE STILL
EXISTING KKK. OUR
GOVERNMENT, THOUGH
KNOWING OF ITS
EXISTENCE, DOESN'T DO
ANYTHING TO COMBAT ITS
GROWING INFLUENCE.
WHEN RADICALISTIC

GROUPS KNOW THAT THEY WON'T BE STOPPED, THEY ATTEMPT TO PUSH FOR THEIR IDEAS TO BE ACCEPTED, AND OFTEN COMMIT CRIMES AND ATROCITIES AGAINST THE GROUPS THEY HATE AND VIEW AS INFERIOR.

WHILST DRUGS CONTINUE TO FLOOD OUR CITIES WITH AN EVER-GROWING POPULATION OF

ADDICTS, OUR GOVERNMENT REFUSES TO DO ANYTHING ABOUT THEM. THEY ALLOW THEM TO CONTINUE LIVING ON THE STREETS, DROPPING DIRTY AND USED NEEDLES ON THE GROUND WHERE ANY DAY, A CHILD OR ANIMAL COULD STEP ON ONE OF THEM AND DEVELOP A DANGEROUS CONDITION WHICH COULD KILL THEM. THE

GOVERNMENT SIMPLY DROPS CARE PACKAGES BUT NEVER TARGETS THE ROOT OF THE PROBLEM. MAYORS ALLOW THEIR CITIES TO BE DESTROYED BY BOTH THESE ADDICTS BUT ALSO LOOTERS AND CRIMINALS. THEY ALLOW DEALERS TO WALK FREE AND CONTINUE FEEDING THE GROWING CRAVING THAT THESE ADDICTS HAVE. ENTIRE STREETS

BECOME FULL OF
HOMELESS
ENCAMPMENTS AND USED
NEEDLES, YET THE
GOVERNMENT CONTINUES
TO TURN A BLIND EYE,
FORCING THE INNOCENT
PEOPLE OF THESE CITIES
TO BE AFFECTED.
MAYORS IN WASHINGTON
AND CALIFORNIA ALLOW
THESE USERS TO USE
THEIR SUBSTANCES
FREELY IN THE OPEN

WITHOUT ATTEMPTING TO INTERFERE AND INSTEAD OF HELPING, THEY ALLOW THESE GROUPS TO EFFECTIVELY DECLARE INDEPENDENCE FROM THE CITIES THEY GOVERN. WITHIN SEATTLE, THE CAPITOL HILL AUTONOMOUS ZONE WAS GIVEN "INDEPENDENCE" BY THE MAYOR AND POLICE WERE BANNED FROM ENTERING. THIS

ONLY ALLOWED CHAOS TO
FESTER LIKE AN
INFECTION THROUGH A
WOUND. MURDER,
LOOTINGS, TRAFFICKING,
AND RAPE DOMINATED
THE ZONE, YET THE
GOVERNMENT OF
SEATTLE DID NOTHING TO
COMBAT THIS. EVEN
TODAY, CHAOS
DOMINATES DUE TO THE
INEFFECTIVENESS OF THE
GOVERNMENT TO COMBAT

CRIME AND HELP THE PEOPLE THEY ARE MEANT TO PROTECT.

MANY ADDICTS SAY THAT THE REASON THEY TURNED TO DRUGS IS BECAUSE THEY LACKED SUPPORT FROM THE GOVERNMENT AND THEIR OWN COMMUNITY. THIS IS WHAT DIVISION DOES TO PEOPLE. IT MAKES THEM DESIRE SOMETHING ELSE

THAT WILL MAKE THEM
FEEL GOOD. THEY DESIRE
CONNECTION YET THEY
ARE REFUSED THAT
RIGHT.

HOMELESS CAMPS
ARE OFTEN DOMINATED
BY VIOLENCE AND DRUGS
AND THESE HOMELESS
PEOPLE ESTABLISH MORE
OF THEM WHEREVER THEY
CAN, SUCH AS OUTSIDE OF
SCHOOLS, RESIDENTIAL

AREAS, AND FREEWAYS.
SOME OF THEM STEAL
FROM STORES OR ROB
PEOPLE JUST SO THEY
CAN AFFORD ANOTHER
HIGH. IT IS SAD THAT THIS
HAPPENS, BUT IT IS
WORSE THAT THE
AVERAGE CIVILIAN MUST
WATCH OUT WHERE THEY
WALK OR ELSE THEY WILL
CATCH A DISEASE FROM A
DIRTY BLADE OR NEEDLE,
OR THEY GET ATTACKED

BY A HOMELESS PERSON
FOR NO REASON. THE
GOVERNMENT CONTINUES
TO LET THIS HAPPEN EVEN
THOUGH IT IS AN OBVIOUS
PROBLEM. EVERYWHERE
YOU GO, THERE IS
SOMETHING TO WATCH
OUT FOR BECAUSE THE
GOVERNMENT DOESN'T
CARE ENOUGH TO HELP
THEIR OWN CIVILIANS OR
BOTHER TO CLEAN THE
MESSES THEY ARE

HELPING CAUSE. THE
OTHER PROBLEM IS MANY
OF THESE HOMELESS
PEOPLE OR ADDICTS
WANT TO REMAIN
HOMELESS BECAUSE THEY
DON'T WANT TO FOLLOW
RULES. SOME OF THESE
PEOPLE CHOOSE TO RUIN
CITIES AND HURT OTHER
PEOPLE BECAUSE THEY
DON'T WANT TO OBEY THE
LAW. ENTIRE
NEIGHBORHOODS GET

DESTROYED EVERYDAY BY
HOMELESS
ENCAMPMENTS. MANY OF
THESE HOMELESS PEOPLE
TURN TO CRIME TO EARN
MONEY TO FUEL EITHER
AN ADDICTION OR
BECAUSE OF NEED. THEY
BREAK INTO CARS AND
STEAL WHATEVER THEY
CAN TAKE. SOME OF THEM
DO DRUGS INSIDE OF
THESE CARS THEY BROKE
INTO.

Activists who think they are doing good for the people are only doing worse. They riot and loot and use their ideals as justification. They use the disparity as justification to commit crime and cause damage and chaos to cities. They choose to use the situation of the poor as

JUSTIFICATION TO HURT
OTHERS. THEY DON'T
CARE ABOUT THE PEOPLE.
THEY ONLY WANT TO
FURTHER THEIR OWN
GOALS ON THE BACKS OF
THE HARD-WORKING
PEOPLE AND THE
STARVING PEOPLE.
ANYBODY WHO VIEWS
SOMETHING DIFFERENTLY
THAN THEM IS INSTANTLY
A THREAT TO THEIR
IDEOLOGY. THEY MAKE

PEOPLE FEAR SPEAKING
OUT AND EXPRESSING
THEIR FREEDOM OF
SPEECH AND EXPRESSION
TO PREVENT OTHERS
FROM EXPOSING THEIR
UNCARING ATTITUDE.

My Experiences

Ever since I grew up, I have been poor, even today my family can barely afford food. We always struggled and still struggle to afford both our bills and daily necessities. When I was twelve, my house and the entire town burnt down in the Caldor Fire, with barely any houses remaining. We were forced to move. This fire could have been stopped but the Californian government under Gavin Newsom began stripping away a key layer of defense from fires by shutting down Inmate Firefighter Programs. He not only

ENDED A REFORM POSSIBILITY FOR PRISONERS BUT ALSO STRIPPED US, MY FAMILY AND MY ENTIRE COMMUNITY OF PROTECTION.

We then lived with my uncle and aunt in their RV for months until a very sweet couple who I will forever be thankful

FOR TOOK US IN AND
OFFERED US HOUSING
INSIDE A RENTAL. WE
LIVED THERE UNTIL WE
MANAGED TO SCROUNGE
UP BARELY ENOUGH
MONEY FOR A HOUSE IN
SACRAMENTO. WITH
CALIFORNIA BECOMING
MORE EXPENSIVE, SOON
WE WON'T BE ABLE TO
STAY HERE ANYMORE BUT
WE ALSO CANNOT
AFFORD TO LEAVE THIS

STATE. BUT ALSO, I DON'T WANT TO LEAVE IT. I HAVE SEEN WHAT HAS HAPPENED TO CALIFORNIA AND I WANT TO CHANGE IT. BUT CHANGE REQUIRES THE BACKING OF A LOT OF PEOPLE. KNOWING THAT THOSE WHO WISH TO CHANGE THINGS OFTEN ARE UNABLE TO DUE TO THE DOMINANCE OF THE REPUBLICAN AND

Democrat parties, we
need to spread our
word, our calls for
change. Voices sound
louder when together
than when a single
man shouts alone.
When the government
fails you, you must
rely on your
neighbors, family, and
community.

When my family, such as my uncle and brother had severe medical issues, my uncle with cancer and my brother with ulcers, not only did they suffer, but their families also suffered. My uncle's family was forced to pay expensive bills for treatment. My family had to do the same.

With healthcare being so expensive, it makes many fear or not want to go to a hospital as they cannot afford treatment. My family's vehicles have been robbed multiple times with windows shattered. One of those times, they broke into my brother's car and left drugs on of the front

SEAT. WE CALLED THE POLICE AND THEY SAID THEY WOULD PATROL OUR NEIGHBORHOOD, BUT WE HAVEN'T SEEN A SINGLE OFFICER SINCE THAT DAY. WE STILL MUST DEAL WITH THESE CRIMINALS ALONE. WE MUST FEAR THAT ONE DAY OUR NEIGHBORHOOD COULD GET SHOT UP OR ONE DAY OUR HOUSE COULD BE

BROKEN INTO BY ARMED CRIMINALS.

The Ouroborist Goal

Ouroborism is built on the idea of preserving the United States by protecting national unity, patriotism, protecting our historic and patriotic relics, and ensuring the rights of affordable healthcare, housing, and the right to feel safe in their country.

It is built on the idea that the poor should not be abandoned by their leaders. It is built on the foundations of a new form of democracy and liberty, that the American people will remain equal and that the United States will become a beacon of hope to the oppressed of the world. No more

WILL THE POOR BE SUBJUGATED BY THE RICH. THE WORKERS WILL GET THEIR FAIR PAY AND THE HOMELESS GET THEIR DESERVED HOME. THE ADDICT GETS REHABILITATED, AND THE CRISIS OF POVERTY, HOMELESSNESS, AND ADDICTION ENDS. NO MORE WILL OUR CHILDREN FEAR FOR THEIR LIVES AT SCHOOL

AND NO MORE WILL PARENTS HAVE TO WORRY ABOUT THEIR CHILDREN'S SAFETY. AMERICANS WILL BE ABLE TO WALK THE STREETS WITHOUT RISK OF BEING ATTACKED. OUR CITIES WILL BECOME BEAUTIFUL ONCE AGAIN AND THE DRUG EMPIRES THAT FORMED AMONG THE DECAYING DEMOCRACY WILL BE DISMANTLED. THE

PRESERVATION OF OUR NATION WILL BE OF THE HIGHEST IMPORTANCE AND PATRIOTISM WILL BECOME POPULAR ONCE AGAIN.

OUR BORDERS SHALL BE PROTECTED TO ENSURE THE PRESERVATION OF OUR SAFETY FROM TERRORISM AND OTHER THREATS TO THE AMERICAN PEOPLE.

THE PEOPLE WILL NO LONGER HAVE TO FEAR ANOTHER ONCOMING DEPRESSION, LOSING THEIR JOB, LOSING THEIR HOME OR LOSING THEIR LIFE IN THE EVENT OF A VIOLENT ATTACK BY AN ADDICT. THE THREAT OF VIOLENCE BETWEEN A DIVIDED AMERICA WILL PASS AND EVERY CIVILIAN WILL BE ABLE TO SPEAK TO THE OTHER SIDE

FREELY WITHOUT
BICKERING BETWEEN THE
TWO. NO MORE WILL
THERE BE A DEEP HATRED
BETWEEN EVERY
NATIONALITY UNDER OUR
FLAG AND OUR
NEWFOUND CULTURE
WILL BECOME A NEW
SYMBOL TO THE WORLD
OF OUR NEWLY
ESTABLISHED AND
REFORMED UNION.

The only way to prevent the further decay of our country is to turn towards the younger political leaders and unite under the newly established parties. Soon, the effects of our current situation will be irreversible, and we will continue to sink further. Our population is

DWINDLING DUE TO THE
LACK OF COMPETENT
LEADERS AND THE POOR
ECONOMY CRIPPLING THE
LIVES OF FAMILIES. THE
PEOPLE CANNOT AFFORD
HOUSING FOR THEIR
CHILDREN AND CANNOT
AFFORD TO FEED THEM,
RESULTING IN OUR
POPULATION
REPLACEMENT RATE
FALLING BELOW THE
REQUIREMENT. IF WE

CONTINUE TO ALLOW THE GOVERNMENT TO OVERCHARGE FAMILIES, OUR COUNTRY WILL CEASE TO EXIST OR WILL CRUMBLE INTO CIVIL WAR. TO PROVIDE FAMILIES AND CHILDREN THE SUITABLE CONDITIONS FOR LIVING, THEY WILL BE GIVEN THE CHANCE TO RECEIVE EMPLOYMENT IN THE FORM OF NEW JOB OPENINGS SPONSORED BY

THE FUTURE Ouroborist
government.

THE INACTION OF THE
JUSTICE SYSTEM TO
SUCCESSFULLY COMBAT
ACTS OF VIOLENCE SUCH
AS DOMESTIC ABUSE, SEX
CRIMES, ANIMAL ABUSE,
CHILD ABUSE AND OTHER
SEVERE CRIMES WILL NO
LONGER OCCUR. THE
JUDGES WHO ACCEPT
BRIBES AND GIVE

CRIMINALS WHO COMMIT THESE VIOLENT AND EVIL ACTS NO PUNISHMENT WILL BE PUNISHED ACCORDINGLY. THE CRIMINAL WHO RECEIVED NO PUNISHMENT OR LITTLE CONSEQUENCE WILL BE PUNISHED TO ENSURE THEY NEVER HURT ANOTHER PERSON AGAIN, AS WELL AS TO ENSURE THE AMERICAN PEOPLE FEEL SAFE AT

NIGHT KNOWING THAT A DANGEROUS CRIMINAL HAS GOTTEN LOCKED UP.

CRIMINAL GANGS WILL BE ABOLISHED, AND ORDER RESTORED IN THEIR WAKE. THE PEOPLE WILL BE ABLE TO LIVE FREELY NOW THAT THEY NO LONGER NEED TO WORRY ABOUT WHETHER THEY WILL BE HOME BY THE END OF THE DAY. FOR

THESE CHANGES TO
HAPPEN, WE MUST ALL
JOIN AND UNITE UNDER
OUROBORISM, AN
IDEOLOGY FOUNDED BY
SOMEBODY WHO KNOWS
HOW IT FEELS TO BE
NEGLECTED BY THE
GOVERNMENT, SOMEBODY
WHO KNOWS HOW IT
FEELS TO BE ONE WITH
THE MASSES. SOMEBODY
WHO CARES ABOUT THE
PEOPLE AND DESIRES

REFORM AND CHANGE.
OUROBORISM IS THE
FOUNDATION OF A NEW
FORM OF DEMOCRACY, A
DEMOCRACY WHICH IS
UPHELD BY THE PEOPLE.

ORDER WILL BE
RESTORED IN OUR
COUNTRY. THOSE WHO
ATTEMPT TO JUSTIFY
THEIR RIOTING AND
VIOLENT ACTIONS
AGAINST THE AMERICAN

PEOPLE WILL BE
PUNISHED. OUR SAFETY IS
MY HIGHEST GOAL, OUR
NATION IS WHAT I PLEDGE
TO FIX. OUR JUSTICE
SYSTEM WILL BE
REPAIRED AND THOSE
WHO PREVIOUSLY ABUSED
THE INNOCENT FOR THEIR
OWN GAIN WILL FACE
CONSEQUENCES. OUR
CHILDREN WILL BE SAFE
AND PROTECTED. OUR
SCHOOL SYSTEMS

REINVIGORATED; OUR
NATION IMPROVED. OLD
VALUES WILL BE
REPLACED WITH NEW
VALUES THAT FIT OUR
NEEDS. CRIMINALS WHO
GET AWAY WITHOUT ANY
PUNISHMENT WILL NOW
FACE PERSECUTION AND
WILL BE LOCKED AWAY TO
NEVER HURT ANOTHER
PERSON EVER AGAIN.
OUR NATURAL BEAUTY
WILL BE PROTECTED

FROM DESTRUCTION AND OUR CRUMBLING AND UGLY CITIES WILL BE REPAIRED AND MADE BEAUTIFUL AGAIN.

THOSE WHO DESIRE TO SPREAD DISSENT AND BURN OUR SYMBOLS OF NATIONAL UNITY AND IDENTITY WILL NOT BE ALLOWED TO CONTINUE THIS. THEY USE "FREEDOM OF

EXPRESSION" AND "FREE SPEECH" TO JUSTIFY THEIR DESTRUCTION OF WHAT MAKES US ALL AMERICAN. THEY URINATE, DEFECATE, BURN, AND SPIT UPON OUR FLAG WHICH REPRESENTS US AS A FREE NATION AND A FREE PEOPLE. THESE PEOPLE THEN CALL FOR THE DIVISION OF OUR NATION AND TEAR DOWN THE

STATUES OF OUR FOUNDERS AND EXPRESS THEIR WISHES TO DESTROY OUR COUNTRY.

THE CURRENT STATE OF OUR NATION IS MAKING IT A BREEDING GROUND FOR SEPARATIST MOVEMENTS AND CRIMINAL ORGANIZATIONS. THESE GROUPS CAUSE DESTRUCTION

THROUGHOUT OUR COUNTRY AND ATTACK WHOEVER OPPOSES THEM. THEY KIDNAP AND TRAFFIC INNOCENT PEOPLE INTO LIVES OF SLAVERY AND SUFFERING. THIS MUST BE STOPPED TO ENSURE THE PRESERVATION OF OUR CIVILIZATION AND TO ENSURE THE RIGHT TO FREEDOM FOR EVERY AMERICAN CIVILIAN.

THE POOR ARE ABUSED BY THE RICH AND POWERFUL, AND THE RICH USE DIRTY TACTICS TO PREVENT THEMSELVES FROM PAYING EQUAL TAXES WHEN IT IS THEM WHO SHOULD PAY MORE THAN THE ORDINARY AMERICAN. THE GOVERNMENT IS COMPLETELY AWARE OF THIS YET REFUSES TO INTERVENE, CAUSING

MORE STRIFE FOR
FAMILIES WHO ARE
UNABLE TO AFFORD TO
PAY THEIR BILLS. THIS ALL
RESULTS IN FAMILIES
STARVING AND PEOPLE
DYING. CORRUPT CITY
OFFICIALS, IN ORDER TO
SAVE MONEY, FIND THE
CHEAPEST ALTERNATIVES
TO FIX AN ISSUE, AND
THESE ALTERNATIVES
OFTEN MAKE THE
PROBLEM WORSE. IN

Flint, Michigan, city
officials changed the
water source without
doing the necessary
inspections, resulting
in lead polluting the
water. Twelve people
were killed by this,
and those officials
were never arrested
even when people
pressured them to be
locked up. This
reveals that the

GOVERNMENT, MEANT TO
SERVE THE PEOPLE AND
PROTECT THEM, ARE
INSTEAD AGAINST THE
PEOPLE AND ONLY WANT
MONEY FOR THEMSELVES.

CORRUPTION IN OUR
MEDICAL INDUSTRY
RESULTS IN THE DEATH OF
HUNDREDS, INCLUDING
CHILDREN. PEOPLE ARE
UNABLE TO AFFORD
TREATMENT, AND SOME

HOSPITALS, WHEN
LEARNING OF THEIR
PATIENTS BEING AN
ORGAN DONOR, DECIDE
TO TAKE THOSE ORGANS
BY FALSELY DECLARING
THE PATIENT DECEASED,
AND KILLING THEM.

OUR VETERANS ARE
MISTREATED AND
NEGLECTED BY THE
GOVERNMENT, RESULTING
IN MANY BECOMING

HOMELESS. THEY ARE UNABLE TO AFFORD PROPER HEALTHCARE SUCH AS THERAPY FOR THEIR EXPERIENCES IN BATTLE AND ARE OFTEN LEFT TO DEAL WITH THEIR ISSUES THEMSELVES. WE SHOULD TREAT OUR VETERANS WITH RESPECT, NOT TREAT THEM AS IF THEY DIDN'T FIGHT FOR THEIR COUNTRY. THESE

VETERANS SHOULD BE
PROVIDED WITH THE
SERVICES THEY NEED.

   HEALTHCARE IS
UNAFFORDABLE FOR THE
AVERAGE AMERICAN.
EVEN WITH INSURANCE,
PAYING THE BILLS IS
OFTEN TOO EXPENSIVE.
EVERY HUMAN DESERVES
THE RIGHT TO
AFFORDABLE
HEALTHCARE, AND

THOUGH OUR NATION IS BUILT ON THE FOUNDATIONS OF LIBERTY, EQUALITY, AND PROVIDING RIGHTS TO THE PEOPLE, WE ARE STILL UNABLE TO AFFORD MEDICAL SUPPLIES AND THE INDUSTRY IS FULL OF DISCRIMINATION. PHARMACEUTICAL COMPANIES OVERPRICE THEIR MEDICINE EVEN WHEN IT TAKES LESS

THAN TEN DOLLARS TO
PRODUCE IT. THE
AVERAGE COST OF
INSULIN IS BETWEEN
FIFTY TO A THOUSAND
DOLLARS EVEN THOUGH IT
COSTS LESS THAN FIVE
DOLLARS TO
MANUFACTURE IT.

PUBLIC SAFETY IS AT
RISK DUE TO THE NUMBER
OF PSYCHOPATHS AND
SOCIOPATHS FREELY

WALKING OUR STREETS, AND AT ANY POINT THEY CAN SNAP. 27% OF HOMICIDES ARE CAUSED BY PSYCHOPATHS AND OVER 70% OF CRIMINALS ARE SOCIOPATHS. DYLAN STORM ROOF, THE MAN WHO COMMITTED THE HORRIFIC CRIME OF THE CHARLESTON CHURCH SHOOTING, IS A SOCIOPATH. NINE PEOPLE WERE KILLED THAT DAY,

AND WE HAVEN'T
LEARNED. ANOTHER
SHOOTING, THE BUFFALO
SHOOTING IN 2022,
RESULTED IN THE DEATH
OF TEN INNOCENT
PEOPLE. PAYTON S.
GENDRON SHOT UP A
BLACK COMMUNITY OVER
HIS HATRED. HE OFTEN
MADE "JOKES" ABOUT
WANTING TO COMMIT
MURDER-SUICIDE OR MASS
SHOOTING WHEN HE WAS

IN HIGH SCHOOL, AND YET
NOTHING WAS DONE EVEN
WHEN HE WAS BROUGHT
IN FOR A PSYCHIATRIC
EVALUATION. WE ALLOW
THESE PEOPLE TO
CONTINUE WALKING THE
STREETS WHEN THEY
POSE A RISK TO THE
SAFETY OF US ALL,
ESPECIALLY OUR
CHILDREN. JULY 4TH, A
DAY MEANT TO SYMBOLIZE
OUR DECLARATION AS A

FREE NATION, A DAY MEANT TO BE JOYFUL, OFTEN TURNS INTO TRAGEDY, AS MONSTERS USE THE LARGE CROWDS TO PLAY OUT THEIR FANTASIES AND COMMIT HORRIFIC SHOOTINGS ON INNOCENT PEOPLE. IN 2023, TWENTY-TWO SHOOTINGS OCCURRED DURING INDEPENDENCE DAY CELEBRATIONS, RESULTING IN THE TRAGIC

LOSS OF TWENTY PEOPLE, AND INJURING 126. THE COLUMBINE SHOOTERS BOTH SUFFERED FROM PSYCHOPATHY, AND THAT RESULTED IN THEM MURDERING FIFTEEN INNOCENT PEOPLE, MOST BEING TEENAGERS. JUSTICE WAS NEVER OFFICIALLY SERVED FOR THE PARENTS OF THOSE WHO WERE LOST. WE MUST WORK TO PREVENT

MORE OF THESE
MASSACRES FROM
HAPPENING. WE MUST
PREVENT MORE INNOCENT
AMERICANS, INCLUDING
CHILDREN FROM BEING
KILLED BY PEOPLE WHO
LACK CARE FOR THEIR
FELLOW HUMAN BEINGS.
MY GOAL IS TO PROTECT
MY FELLOW AMERICANS,
AND WITH THE SUPPORT
OF THE PEOPLE, THAT
CAN BE ACHIEVED.

Unemployment is on the rise as workers are fired or replaced. Not only does this affect the individual, but it also affects their families, resulting in starvation and homelessness. To solve this issue, Ouroborism encourages the formation of more

STABLE EMPLOYMENT
OPTIONS, AS WELL AS
BUILD NEW EMPLOYMENT
OPPORTUNITIES FROM
PRE-EXISTING
ORGANIZATIONS,
ALLOWING FOR THE
ORDINARY AMERICAN TO
RECEIVE A JOB. TO
PROTECT BUSINESS
OWNERS AND THE
AVERAGE AMERICAN
FROM BANKRUPTCY OR
DEBT, STRICT

CRACKDOWNS ON CORRUPTION WITHIN INSURANCE AGENCIES WILL BE CONDUCTED TO ENSURE NO INNOCENT MAN OR WOMAN IS ABUSED BY THEIR INSURANCE AGENT, AND THAT THEY CAN AFFORD TO SURVIVE. SOON, TRUST CAN BE PUT INTO A NATIONAL INSURANCE AGENCY THAT WILL BE COMPLETELY PURGED OF

ALL CORRUPTION,
PROTECTING THE
AMERICAN PEOPLE FROM
THOSE WHO DO NOT CARE
ABOUT THEM.

HOMELESSNESS WILL
BE SOLVED AS
OUROBORISM
ENCOURAGES THE
CONSTRUCTION OF
AFFORDABLE HOUSING
FOR THOSE WHO ARE
UNABLE TO AFFORD IT,

WHILST ALSO GIVING THESE HOMELESS CITIZENS NEW JOBS IN OUROBORIST FUNDED ESTABLISHMENTS, SUCH AS TOWARDS AGRICULTURAL AND INDUSTRIAL SECTORS TO MAKE PRODUCTION AND THE SALE OF GOODS CHEAPER, NOT ONLY HELPING THE UNEMPLOYED, BUT ALSO HELPING THE POOR.

We must support our allies in their times of need as every war brings our personal freedoms at stake. If we refuse to provide aid to our allies in times of war by providing them with equipment, it could lead to a domino effect, where if one falls, the rest will go down with them. Not

ONLY WILL INTERVENTION
PREVENT FOREIGN
COUNTRIES FROM
OVERSTEPPING THEIR
BOUNDARIES INTO OUR
SPHERES OF INFLUENCE,
BUT IT WILL ALSO
PROVIDE JOBS, AS
WORKERS WILL BE
NEEDED TO PRODUCE
MORE EQUIPMENT,
ENDING THE
UNEMPLOYMENT CRISIS,
AS WELL AS ENSURING

OUR FREEDOM AND
NATION ARE PROTECTED
FROM GREEDY AND EVIL
EYES. INNOCENT
CIVILIANS ARE
MASSACRED BY
SOCIOPATHIC AND
GENOCIDAL RUSSIAN
FORCES. VIDEOS EXIST
WHERE RUSSIAN
INFANTRY AND RUSSIAN
BACKED MERCENARIES
KILL INNOCENTS IN
EXTREMELY HORRIFIC

WAYS. TANKS BLOW UP GROUPS OF CIVILIANS, AND SOLDIERS' GUN DOWN FLEEING CITIZENS. RUSSIAN ARTILLERY BOMBARDS HOSPITALS AND CIVILIAN CENTERS SUCH AS APARTMENTS. OVER 10,000 CIVILIANS HAVE PERISHED, INCLUDING OVER 590 CHILDREN IN THIS BRUTAL WAR, YET IT STILL RAGES ON. THOSE INNOCENT

PEOPLE COULD HAVE LIVED LONG LIVES, AND COULD HAVE DONE GREAT THINGS, YET THEY WERE CUT SHORT BY MANIACS. SOMETIMES, INTERVENTION REQUIRES MEN TO BE SENT TO BATTLE, AND THOSE MEN MAY DIE, BUT THEY WOULD HAVE DIED TO PROTECT AMERICA AND ITS PEOPLE, AS WELL AS VICTIMS OF GENOCIDE

AND TERRORISM.
AMERICA IS STRONG, BUT
STRENGTH CAN ALWAYS
CONTINUE TO BUILD UP,
AND STRENGTH WILL
MAKE OTHERS QUESTION
WHETHER THEY DESIRE
CONFLICT. RUSSIAN
SOLDIERS TAUNT US AND
OUR ALLIES WITH OUR
CAPTURED EQUIPMENT,
EQUIPMENT THAT
AMERICAN SWEAT AND
BLOOD MANUFACTURED.

LXXXV

EQUIPMENT USED
AGAINST US BY AN
ENEMY. REVENGE
THROUGH CONFLICT IS
SOMETIMES NEEDED TO
PUT PEOPLE IN THEIR
PLACE, AND IN THIS CASE,
IT WOULDN'T JUST BE
REVENGE, BUT ALSO
VENGEANCE.

WAR IS SOMETIMES
NECESSARY TO ENSURE
THE SURVIVAL OF LIBERTY

AND FREEDOM AS WELL
AS THE AMERICAN
PEOPLE. CONFLICT MADE
OUR NATION FREE, AND
CONFLICT CAN BE USED
TO DESTROY WHAT IS
CURRENTLY DESTROYING
OUR COUNTRY FROM THE
INSIDE. CARTELS KILL
HUNDREDS OF INNOCENTS
EVERY MONTH IN MEXICO,
AND THEIR DRUGS KILL
THOUSANDS OF
INNOCENTS EVERY DAY IN

AMERICA. MEXICO IS
UNABLE TO COMBAT
THEIR CORRUPTION AND
INTERNAL ISSUES AND
ALLOW CAPTURED
CARTEL LEADERS TO GO
FREE WITHOUT A FIGHT.
THEIR MARINES ARE THE
ONLY COMPETENT AND
TRULY INDEPENDENT
ARMY WITHIN. MEXICO'S
MILITARY AND POLICE ARE
ALL ON THE PAYROLL OF
ALL THE CARTELS, AND

THOSE WHO AREN'T ARE
EXECUTED AND
TORTURED. MEXICO
CONTINUES TO ALLOW
THIS ALL TO HAPPEN DUE
TO THEIR GOVERNMENTS
UNWILLINGNESS TO
PROVIDE PROPER
RESISTANCE. AMERICA
MUST APPLY PRESSURE
TO PROTECT INNOCENT
LIVES, AND IT HASN'T.
OUROBORISM WILL BE
ABLE TO PROTECT THE

United States. It can provide reform and change to the country. It will prevent the innocent from being harmed by incompetency and corruption. It will ensure order is restored and division among America ended. ··Our nation will soon be too far gone to allow for us to repair

IT, BUT IF WE MAKE A
CHANGE NOW, IT CAN BE
SAVED, AND THE
*AMERICAN DREAM
RESTORED*.